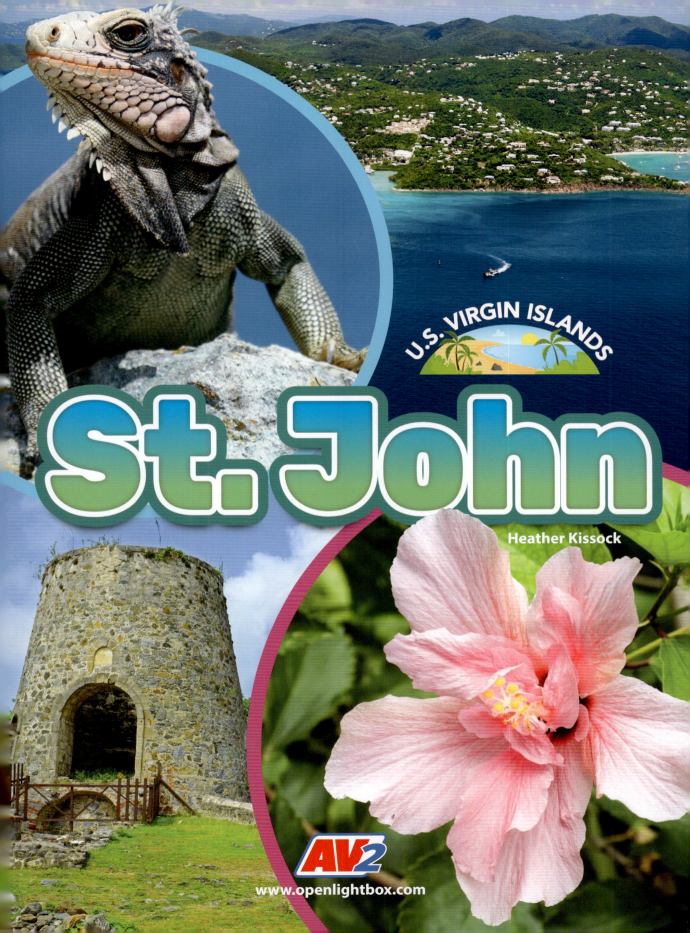

U.S. VIRGIN ISLANDS

St. John

Heather Kissock

AV2

www.openlightbox.com

Step 1
Go to www.openlightbox.com

Step 2
Enter this unique code
DKOTJ061M

Step 3
Explore your interactive eBook!

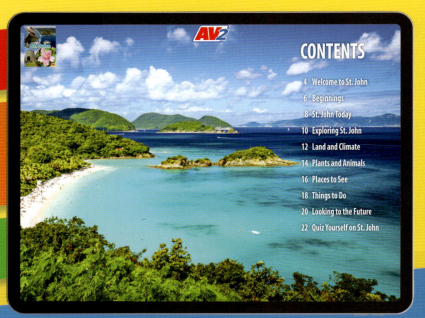

AV2 is optimized for use on any device

Your interactive eBook comes with…

Contents
Browse a live contents page to easily navigate through resources

Audio
Listen to sections of the book read aloud

Videos
Watch informative video clips

Weblinks
Gain additional information for research

Slideshows
View images and captions

Try This!
Complete activities and hands-on experiments

Key Words
Study vocabulary, and complete a matching word activity

Quizzes
Test your knowledge

Share
Share titles within your Learning Management System (LMS) or Library Circulation System

Citation
Create bibliographical references following APA, CMOS, and MLA styles

This title is part of our AV2 digital subscription

1-Year Grades K–5 Subscription
ISBN 978-1-7911-3320-7

Access hundreds of AV2 titles with our digital subscription.
Sign up for a FREE trial at www.openlightbox.com/trial

The digital components of this book are guaranteed to stay active for at least five years from the date of publication.

U.S. VIRGIN ISLANDS

St. John

CONTENTS

2	Interactive eBook Code
4	Welcome to St. John
6	Beginnings
8	St. John Today
10	Exploring St. John
12	Land and Climate
14	Plants and Animals
16	Places to See
18	Things to Do
20	Looking to the Future
22	Quiz Yourself on St. John
23	Key Words/Index

WELCOME TO
St. John

Virgin Islands National Park covers more than **65 percent** of St. John.

St. John is home to more than **400 wild donkeys**.

There is only **one way** to reach St. John, and that is by boat. The island does not have an airport.

4 U.S. Virgin Islands

About 1,100 miles (1,770 kilometers) southeast of the U.S. state of Florida lies an **archipelago** of more than 50 islands. These islands belong to the United States, although they are not part of a state. Called the United States Virgin Islands, they are one of the country's many **territories**. St. Croix, St. John, and St. Thomas are the archipelago's three principal islands.

St. John is the smallest of the three main islands. Like many places in the Caribbean, St. John is known for its white-sand beaches and warm weather. Much of the island is a national park. This means that it has remained mostly untouched by humans.

St. John 5

Beginnings

St. John is actually part of an underwater mountain range. This range began to form about 100 million years ago, when volcanic activity in the area caused Earth's **tectonic plates** to collide. Some of the rock pushed upward, forming mountains. As the mountains rose above the water, their peaks and ridges became islands. St. John is one of these islands.

Researchers have found Taino artifacts at St. John's Cinnamon Bay that indicate the site was used for ancient ceremonies.

People did not begin to live on the island until about 770 BC. No one is sure where these first peoples came from. What is known is that they survived by fishing and gathering plants. In about 200 AD, people from South America arrived on St. John. They began to farm the land.

By 1200, an **Indigenous** people known as the Taino were living on St. John. When Italian explorer Christopher Columbus arrived on the island in 1493, he encountered them there. Europeans began to use the Virgin Islands to grow crops such as sugarcane, cotton, and tobacco. St. John, and other nearby islands, became the property of Denmark. The islands remained under Danish rule until 1917, when Denmark sold them to the United States.

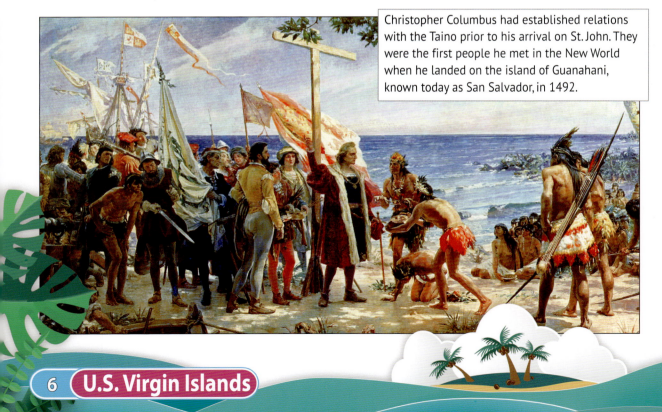

Christopher Columbus had established relations with the Taino prior to his arrival on St. John. They were the first people he met in the New World when he landed on the island of Guanahani, known today as San Salvador, in 1492.

6 U.S. Virgin Islands

St. John Timeline

770s BC
St. John's first inhabitants arrive.

200 AD
People from South America settle on St. John and use the land to grow crops.

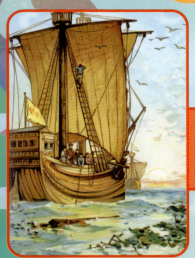

1200 to 1500
The Taino arrive on St. John and eventually become its main Indigenous group.

1493
Christopher Columbus explores the area now known as the Virgin Islands.

1675
After laying claim to St. Thomas, Denmark also assumes control of St. John.

1917
The United States purchases the U.S. Virgin islands from Denmark for $25 million.

1952
Virgin Islands National Park is established on St. John.

2024
St. John's Trunk Bay is voted the world's best beach in an annual travel survey.

St. John

St. John Today

Approximately 4,000 people currently call St. John home. This is about 4 percent of the total U.S. Virgin Islands' population. The island's small size and the amount of land taken up by the national park are the main reasons for the limited number of people living there.

Most of the people who live on St. John have an Afro-Caribbean background. English is the island's official language, but it is often spoken in a variety of Caribbean **dialects**. Spanish and Creole can also be heard on St. John.

Cruz Bay offers tourists a variety of shopping opportunities, ranging from malls to street vendors.

Most of St. John's people live in **one of two communities**—Coral Bay or Cruz Bay.

St. John has a total of **five grocery stores.**

The population of St. John has **decreased** by about **300 people** in the last **10 years.**

8 U.S. Virgin Islands

St. John's residents are known for their friendly, welcoming nature. As tourism is the island's main industry, they are always willing to help visitors find places to eat, sleep, and experience island life. Other industries important to the island include agriculture and **services**.

St. John's warm weather ensures that visitors have their choice of outdoor dining venues.

Exploring St. John

St. John lies about 3 miles (5 km) east of St. Thomas and about 40 miles (64 km) north of St. Croix. It is the island closest to the British Virgin Islands, another archipelago located northeast of the U.S. territory. St. John measures just 9 miles (14 km) long and 5 miles (8 km) wide. It covers an area of about 20 square miles (52 square kilometers).

Cruz Bay
With a population of about 2,800, Cruz Bay is St. John's largest town. It is also considered to be the island's capital. Most of St. John's restaurants, hotels, and shops are found here.

Bordeaux Mountain
Rising to a height of 1,277 feet (390 meters), Bordeaux Mountain is the highest point in all of St. John. The mountain is found within the borders of Virgin Islands National Park. People can hike to its summit.

10 U.S. Virgin Islands

Virgin Islands National Park

St. John's national park was a gift from American millionaire Laurance Rockefeller. The owner of most of St. John's land, he donated much of it to the U.S. government for the creation of a park. Virgin Islands National Park covers an area of 23 square miles (60 sq. km). This includes Coral Reef National Monument, an underwater nature **reserve**.

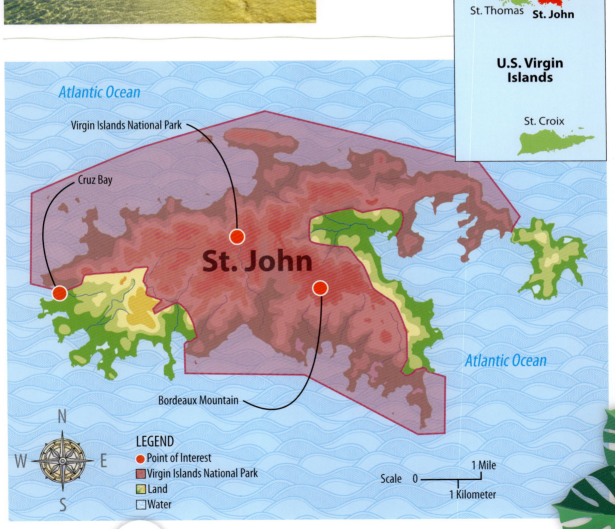

Land and Climate

One of St. John's key attractions are its beaches. Even though St. John is a small island, it still has more than 30 of them. These stretches of white sand are scattered along the island's rugged coastline. Some are in open areas, while others are hidden within quiet coves.

The interior of St. John is a combination of hills and valleys. Very little of the island is flat. Tropical forests cover much of its land.

The beach at Trunk Bay is one of the longer beaches on St. John. It extends for about 528 yards (482 m).

12 U.S. Virgin Islands

While St. John is surrounded by water, there are no lakes or rivers on the island itself. A series of small streams and springs can be found on St. John's south side. However, they are not a reliable water supply. Residents needing fresh water must store rainwater, dig wells, or purchase water brought in from other places.

St. John has moderate to high temperatures year-round. Its average low is 79° Fahrenheit (26° Celsius), while its average high is 82°F (28°C). This warmth extends to the waters around the island. Their temperature averages about 82°F (28°C) as well. August, September, and October are the island's hottest months. The coolest temperatures arrive in February and March. Most of St. John's precipitation falls between August and November.

Average High Temperatures

JAN	79°F (26°C)
FEB	79°F (26°C)
MAR	79°F (26°C)
APR	80°F (26.5°C)
MAY	83°F (28°C)
JUN	83°F (28°C)
JUL	83°F (28°C)
AUG	84°F (29°C)
SEP	84°F (29°C)
OCT	84°F (29°C)
NOV	83°F (28°C)
DEC	81°F (27°C)

St. John averages about 45 inches (114 centimeters) of rain per year. Rainfall typically arrives in the form of brief showers in the morning or evening.

St. John 13

Plants and Animals

St. John is home to a wide variety of plants and animals. The island's warm weather makes it an ideal place for tropical trees and flowers. This vegetation provides food and shelter for animals, including **reptiles**, birds, and **mammals**.

Beach Maho
The beach maho is a common shoreline tree in St. John. It is best-known for its heart-shaped leaves. The tree produces yellow flowers that turn purple over time.

Frangipani
Frangipani is a common tropical plant. While the frangipani of other countries may come in a variety of colors, St. John's native plant has a white bloom. No matter where it grows, frangipani is known for its fragrant perfume.

Bananaquit

The bananaquit is the official bird of the U.S. Virgin Islands. These small, yellow-breasted birds are typically found in or near St. John's forested areas. Known for their high-pitched squeaks, they are often heard before they are seen.

Bats

Bats are the only mammals native to St. John and the other U.S. Virgin Islands. In total, six different types can be found here. Most feed on insects and nectar. However, one species is known to eat fish.

Green Iguana

Known for its brightly colored scales, the green iguana is St. John's most common reptile. These lizards can often be seen sunbathing on the island's beaches and rocks. They can grow up to 6 feet (1.8 m) in length.

St. John 15

Places to See

St. John offers visitors many sightseeing opportunities. Some attractions are connected to the island's history. Others showcase its culture.

While no Taino remain on St. John, their presence can still be felt through the art they left behind. A series of **petroglyphs** can be found along Reef Bay Trail, on the southern side of the island. The carvings include faces, symbols, and other designs.

Most visitors to St. John arrive by passenger ferry from St. Thomas. These ferries bring passengers right to Cruz Bay's main commercial area.

It is believed that the Reef Bay petroglyphs were carved between 900 and 1500 AD.

St. John's oldest petroglyph is estimated to be about **2,000 years old.**

At its peak, St. John had **25 sugar plantations** in operation.

The St. John Carnival lasts for **about 1 month.** Most of the action takes place on the **last 5 days.**

16 U.S. Virgin Islands

During **colonial** times, Europeans used St. John mainly as a place to produce sugar. They built large farms called plantations and brought **slaves** from Africa to harvest sugarcane and turn it into sugar. Today, people can visit the ruins of two of these plantations. The Annaberg Plantation features the remains of an old windmill, a sugar factory, and the slave quarters. The Cinnamon Bay plantation has similar structures, as well as the remains of the owner's estate.

The windmill at the Annaberg Plantation was once the tallest windmill in all the Virgin Islands. Built between 1810 and 1830, it measures about 40 feet (12 m) in height.

Slavery was abolished on St. John, and the other U.S. Virgin Islands, on July 3, 1848. Today, islanders commemorate this event with the annual St. John Carnival. Celebrations are held across the island and include traditional music, dances, and foods. Communities also honor American Independence Day as part of the festivities.

Caribbean music is played at many St. John festivals, with local musicians demonstrating their skill on a variety of traditional instruments, including the steel drum.

Things to Do

With tropical waters on all sides and a national park covering most of its surface, St. John offers numerous activities for outdoor enthusiasts. The ability to commune with nature is a major draw for the island. People from across the globe come to St. John to experience its natural wonders.

St. John's many beaches offer visitors the chance to relax, but some also serve as a starting point for snorkeling adventures. The snorkeling in Trunk Bay, on the eastern side of the island, is considered among the world's best. The bay's waters are part of Coral Reef National Monument. The underwater reserve includes a snorkeling trail that allows visitors to view colorful coral reefs, tropical fish, and sea turtles.

St. John offers a variety of boat excursions. Sailboat, catamaran, and motorboat tours all give visitors the chance to view the coastline and St. John's underwater world.

Snorkelers may encounter jellyfish in the waters around St. John. The moon jellyfish is the most common, but other types sometimes make an appearance.

Many people venture to the western side of the island to kayak in the blue waters of Caneel Bay. A variety of sea animals can be encountered in this area. Stingrays and barracudas glide through the waters, while marine birds fly overhead.

People wanting to kayak around St. John can either join an organized tour or rent a kayak and make their own plans.

Hikers of all skill levels will find many trails to explore in Virgin Islands National Park. Some take people past historic sites. Others lead to views of the ocean. A few even delve deep into the jungle, allowing hikers to view the island's plants and animals up close.

St. John's wild donkeys are a common sight on hiking paths. Brought to St. John to help farmers, the animals are now free-roaming and can be found in small herds throughout the island.

St. John 19

Looking to the Future

To many people, St. John may seem like a tropical island paradise. However, it is not completely problem-free. As favorable as the island's location appears to be, it also sits in the path of strong storm systems.

In 2017, St. John was hit with a major hurricane. Nicknamed Irma, the hurricane struck on September 6 and brought island-wide destruction. Trees were uprooted, telephone and power lines were brought down, and buildings were torn apart. Another storm, Hurricane Maria, arrived within two weeks, bringing high winds and flooding. St. John was left devastated. All the features that attracted tourists were either in need of repair or had to be entirely rebuilt.

The rebuilding process was grueling. Immediately after Irma hit, the U.S. government sent the military and other specialists to assist in the cleanup. Unfortunately, they were all **evacuated** when news of Maria's strength was received. It was not until after Maria had moved on that restoration of the island could properly begin. People went to work clearing debris and returning boats and other property to where they belonged. **Infrastructure** projects began to make the island livable again. Virgin Islands National Park was able to reopen 105 days after Irma struck. Most of the island's power was restored before Christmas.

Hurricane Irma caused more than $10 billion in damages across the Caribbean. St. John was one of the islands most impacted.

U.S. Virgin Islands

One of the first priorities of St. John's recovery effort was ensuring that people had food and water. The military played a key role in getting supplies to the island.

PROBLEM SOLVER

St. John's 2017 hurricanes showed that it can be difficult to recover from a natural disaster. What processes and policies could be put in place to overcome this problem?

St. John's local officials were intent on ensuring the island was more prepared for hurricanes in the future. When planning St. John's restoration, they worked to make the new infrastructure better than before. Where possible, power and telephone lines were put underground so that high winds would not impact their use. Steel beams and reinforced concrete were used in the construction of new buildings to give them more stability. If another hurricane were to strike St. John, the island planned to be ready.

St. John 21

QUIZ YOURSELF ON

St. John

1
How much of St. John does Virgin Islands National Park cover?

2
When did the first people arrive on St. John?

3
Approximately how many people live on St. John today?

4
What mountain is St. John's highest point?

5
What are the only mammals native to St. John?

6
When was slavery abolished on St. John?

7
How many beaches does St. John have?

8
When did Hurricane Irma hit St. John?

ANSWERS: 1. More than 65 percent **2.** About 770 BC **3.** 4,000 **4.** Bordeaux Mountain **5.** Bats **6.** July 3, 1848 **7.** More than 30 **8.** September 6, 2017

22 **U.S. Virgin Islands**

Key Words

archipelago: a group of islands

colonial: relating to the ownership of one country by another

dialects: forms of a language spoken in specific parts of a country

evacuated: removed from a place of danger

Indigenous: relating to a country's original, or native, people

infrastructure: the basic systems and services, such as roads and power plants, serving an area

mammals: animals that have a backbone, hair or fur, and feed their young milk

petroglyphs: artwork that is carved directly into a rock's surface

reptiles: cold-blooded animals that have a backbone, lay eggs, and have a body that is covered with scales

reserve: an area of land that is kept in its natural state

services: work that does not produce a physical product

slaves: people who are legally owned by someone else and have to work for that person

tectonic plates: large slabs of rock that make up the surface of Earth

territories: lands that are controlled by a particular country or ruler

Index

animals 4, 14, 15, 18, 19, 22

beaches 5, 7, 12, 18, 22
Bordeaux Mountain 10, 11, 22
British Virgin Islands 10

Caneel Bay 19
Caribbean Sea 5
Columbus, Christopher 6, 7
Coral Bay 8
Coral Reef National Monument 11, 18
Cruz Bay 8, 10, 11, 16

Denmark 6, 7

Florida 5
forests 12, 15, 19

Hurricane Irma 20, 21, 22
Hurricane Maria 20

languages 8

petroglyphs 16
plantations 16, 17
plants 6, 14, 17, 19
precipitation 13

Rockefeller, Laurance 11

slavery 17, 22
snorkeling 18
St. Croix 5, 10, 11
St. John Carnival 16, 17
St. Thomas 5, 7, 10, 11, 16

Taino 6, 7, 16
Trunk Bay 7, 12, 18

United States 5, 6, 7

Virgin Islands National Park 4, 5, 7, 8, 10, 11, 18, 19, 20, 22

Get the best of both worlds.
AV2 bridges the gap between print and digital.

The expandable resources toolbar enables quick access to content including **videos**, **audio**, **activities**, **weblinks**, **slideshows**, **quizzes**, and **key words**.

Animated videos make static images come alive.

Resource icons on each page help readers to further **explore key concepts**.

Published by Lightbox Learning Inc.
276 5th Avenue
Suite 704 #917
New York, NY 10001
Website: www.openlightbox.com

Copyright ©2026 Lightbox Learning Inc.
All rights reserved. No part of this publication may be reproduced, stored in a retrieval system, or transmitted in any form or by any means, electronic, mechanical, photocopying, recording, or otherwise, without the prior written permission of the publisher.

Library of Congress Cataloging-in-Publication Data
Names: Kissock, Heather, author.
Title: St. John / Heather Kissock.
Other titles: Saint John
Description: New York, NY : Lightbox Learning Inc., [2026] | Series: U.S. Virgin Islands | Includes index. | Audience: Grades 2-3
Identifiers: LCCN 2024047649 (print) | LCCN 2024047650 (ebook) | ISBN 9798874507381 (library binding) | ISBN 9798874511562 (paperback) | ISBN 9798874507398 (ebook other) | ISBN 9798874507411 (ebook other)
Subjects: LCSH: Saint John (United States Virgin Islands)--Juvenile literature.
Classification: LCC F2098 .K57 2026 (print) | LCC F2098 (ebook) | DDC 917.297/22--dc23/eng/20250102
LC record available at https://lccn.loc.gov/2024047649
LC ebook record available at https://lccn.loc.gov/2024047650

Printed in Guangzhou, China
1 2 3 4 5 6 7 8 9 0 29 28 27 26 25

032025
101124

Project Coordinator: Heather Kissock
Designer: Terry Paulhus

Photo Credits
Every reasonable effort has been made to trace ownership and to obtain permission to reprint copyright material. The publisher would be pleased to have any errors or omissions brought to its attention so that they may be corrected in subsequent printings. The publisher acknowledges Getty Images, Alamy, Bridgeman Images, and Shutterstock as its primary image suppliers for this title.